Cashing Out

How to Get Cash Out of Your Business While Keeping Operational Control and Maintain Majority Ownership

Scott Ford and David Ryan

Cashing Out

Published by:
90-Minute Books
302 Martinique Drive
Winter Haven, FL 33884
www.90minutebooks.com

For more information on 90-Minute Books including finding out how you can
publish your own lead generating book, visit www.90minutebooks.com or call (863)
318-0464

Here's What's Inside...

Why More Business Owners
Don't Have Financial Freedom 1

The E-Recap Process That Lets You Cash Out
While Maintaining Operational Control 3

How The E-Recap Process
Works for Different Businesses 7

How E-Recap Differs from
Private Equity and ESOP 11

How Much Is Enough? 15

Is Financial Freedom Closer
Than You Think? 19

Mistakes Business Owners
Make Cashing Out...20

Is an E-Recap Right for You? 22

What If You Could Take Significant
Cash Out of Your Business While
Maintaining Majority Ownership? 23

Introduction

Small and medium sized businesses are the financial engine to any country's economy. There are over 30 million small businesses in the US and over 250 million small businesses globally. At least 75% of those businesses do not know what their business is worth, according to the Small Business Association. Most small business owners have achieved financial independence by earning enough to meet their needs. However, a large majority of business owners are unable to achieve true financial freedom without taking assets from their business. Our definition of financial freedom allows entrepreneurs to find balance in their lives and to contribute to the causes they care most about. Too often, we see business owners not able to leverage the worth of their business, which would allow them the financial freedom they crave.

In John Bogle's book titled Enough, Kurt Vonnegut informs his pal Joseph Heller that their host, the hedge fund manager, had made more money in a single day than Heller had earned from his wildly popular novel Catch-22 over its whole history. Heller responded, "Yes, but I have something he will never have - Enough." Most business owners cannot tell you how much they need because they are not clear on their number. We have seen business owners lose everything, their family, and their health all in the pursuit of "more." When business owners have a clear vision for their financial independence and have a plan to cash out, it allows them to create the true financial independence they are looking for.

Enjoy the book!

We hope this book educates you on how to create liquidity for your business, while maintaining equity and operational control. We hope this book inspires you to create a balanced and fulfilled life.

To Your Success!

Scott Ford & David Ryan

Why More Business Owners Don't Have Financial Freedom

The Small Business Association states that lack of business valuation knowledge and financial knowledge are the top two issues facing small businesses today. The reason more business owners do not have the financial freedom they crave comes down to one word: Procrastination.

Having said that, it is very reasonable to procrastinate in this particular area. We will give you an example. Years ago, in 1995, Scott developed an idea that he called the six pillars of life. This happened when his son was diagnosed with a heart condition and needed surgery at the age of six months old; it really put in perspective what is important in life. At that time, he developed what he called six pillars of life, which are: spiritual life, family life, health, career, philanthropy, and then lastly finances.

When looking at these six pillars of focus and responsibility, it's easy to see why most business owners procrastinate on their finances, and it creates a real concern. Most of the wealth of business owners is tied to their business. They started in business to have more freedom and control; and yet now they feel trapped in the business they started to gain freedom. They are spending most of their time on the treadmill we call business instead of trying to live a balanced, fulfilled life. They may have successful companies but now they are around 10 to 15 years older and need to diversify that to spend more time away from the business.

How Much Will Financial Freedom Cost?

Business owners are not always aware of where they are or what they need to have in order to attain that financial freedom. That is why we try to kindly push our clients and business owners to work with a wealth advisor before they take action to sell their business or to recapitalize it, so that they know where they are headed. A wealth adviser can help a business owner understand the financial resources needed to pursue that financial freedom.

Business owners often think the only choice they have is to sell the business; with their personal identity tied up in the business, it is no longer only a business, it is their baby. If they sell the business, they are giving up that control. A great deal of energy has gone into that business, often at the expense of their family life or at the expense of their health.

The E-Recap Process That Lets You Cash Out While Maintaining Operational Control

What does it mean for business owners if they are able to have the freedom and maintain operational control? It means taking considerable cash from the business to live your life the way you want now, instead of waiting for retirement, which we do not have a guarantee that we are going to live to see. It also means finding real balance.

What is Financial Freedom?

An example would be having the resources and time to live life on your terms throughout your career, before your family and health suffer. By cashing out, you can take some chips off the table, diversify your family's wealth, and find the time to pursue what is most important to you.

Another example would allow owners to get personal liquidity in order to diversify their assets, while maintaining equity control and operational autonomy. That is a big deal; as business owners and entrepreneurs, we have typically built this on our own, and while most may want to diversify their assets, they do not want to give up control. The key is taking enough chips off the table so you can attain the amount of money needed to be truly being financially free and independent.

What are the Advantages of Cashing Out?

One unexpected plus is that you may see more growth because you are bringing in a third party that has unique capabilities that you do not have. Another key element business owners and entrepreneurs overlook is diversifying your time as an entrepreneur to spend more time on your passions and things that rejuvenate you. The irony is, balance leads to growth and growth leads to balance. It's a virtuous cycle many entrepreneurs and business owners miss out on, but it is very powerful.

We often ask the business owner what we call the ultimate question. The ultimate question is, "If you went to bed tonight and didn't wake up tomorrow morning, is the company that you have in place today the company you would want handling those services for your family and your love ones?"

Hopefully the answer is yes, but that is not always the case. If it is not, by freeing up and diversifying assets and bringing in a third party with more capabilities, it will allow you to answer that question with a resounding yes. Whether managing your family's wealth or whatever business you are in, you need to be able to answer that question with an undoubtable yes.

How Does E-Recap Offer More Freedom?

Many opportunities are out there for business owners to reach that financial freedom, but it often comes with personal guarantees. We are talking about a system that is free of personal guarantee, so the money is truly outside of the business and outside of those risks that are associated with the business.

Otherwise, it becomes a false financial freedom because they have only doubled up on the leverage of the business, not diversified. Once business owners reach that level and are maintaining operational control, they are more open to looking at the next 5, 10, 15 years where they will ultimately have to retire to allow in the next level of management.

How Does an E-Recap Add Value to the Business?

With an E-Recap, they can bring in an institutional minority partner into the business and help the business upgrade itself; this allows the next generation and the next group of managers to try new products and keep the business healthy and vibrant. That is how you reach that financial freedom while maintaining the control.

The reason we are so passionate about this process is that we can help the owner get over 70% of the value of their business out currently and still have 75% control. That means they are going to have operational control and equity control, because they are going to own the majority of that business. Most business owners we speak with are open to this concept, but they tell us "it sounds too good to be true".

One Typical Example

Let us walk through a typical situation. If you know you have five to seven years before you want to retire, you know how possible it is for a life changing event to occur during that five and seven years, with inside risk as well as outside risk. It is important to deleverage that personal risk, to increase the business value.

If a business owner is approaching retirement, and they have 80% of their net worth tied up in the business, they are going to operate it differently than when they started and had nothing to lose. By taking the cash off the table, the business owner is then able to operate safely; they have their financial freedom, so they can be aggressive and grow like they want without it being a place of risk to their net worth. When you see the economics of both sides in the long term, the business owners are better able to understand and accept it.

How The E-Recap Process Works for Different Businesses

Scott had a friend who had a liquidity event about a year and a half ago. Scott wanted to figure out what was going on. What caused that? What story was Scott's friend and his partner telling themselves or what was being played in their mind throughout their days before they sold? Their comment was that they were not really thinking about it. They planned to do continue doing what they had done forever in their business, but one partner had an unexpected health event.

From that health event he thought "You know, life is short, and I better be making some plans." The partner wanted to move on and follow his passion in life, which happened to be golf. Scott's friend needed to buyout his partner and would need to continue to run the business by himself but in the end he did not want to take more financial risk and risk the personally wealth and financial security he had built for his family. The team members inside the company did not have the capital to buy the company, so he ended up selling the majority of the business to a private equity firm and taking minority interest in the company he founded, and since then that firm has gone public, so it has been successful.

The point is, there was a triggering event, and doing what we are suggesting never crossed his mind. Had it crossed his mind, we think it would have been very well received, because it is what he was looking for. He wanted to maintain majority ownership and control but did not think he could.

Why Aren't Business Owners Aware of This Option?

This approach is new to the smaller businesses from $10 to $50 million in value. This process has long been available to business valued over $50 million, but because of the current economic situation, people looking for quality transactions to invest in, it is now offered to smaller companies.

How Does the Process Work?

Most businesses are measured by EBITDA; EBITDA means Earnings before Interest Taxes Depreciation and Amortization. If we take a business that has two million dollars' worth of EBITDA, and use a five multiple for value, that would give us a business value of $10 million. We would put in a combination of debt and equity, and business owners and their team of professionals would participate in determining what the right balance would be.

For example, in this scenario, we take two million dollars and use a three multiple, and that will produce six million dollars' worth of debt. Now we have six million dollars of debt on this company. We subtract that from the enterprise value of $10 million, which would then leave equity of four million dollars. We would sell 25% of that equity, to raise seven million dollars of value from the company.

You have the six million from the debt, one million because we sold 25% of the net equity, and that money can go out to the owners, free of recourse. That is their money.

It is no longer subject to the risk of the business. At the end of the day, they are going to roll over three million dollars' worth of value while still maintaining 75% ownership, and they have an institution that owns 25%.

One of the things that we try very hard to do is acquire the debt from the same person that we are selling the equity to. That way, everyone's purpose is in alignment, because the people that lent you the money now have equity in your company; it really simplifies the process of getting this money versus other types of transactions. With those seven million dollars, we can measure it to see if that really achieves their financial freedom.

What Are the Most Important Benefits?

The E-Recap Process is all about business owners being able to meet both personal and professional financial goals. They can have asset diversification; they can have succession planning in place, and also have growth opportunities moving forward with their company.

One of the things that we have seen by bringing in the institutional partners is it increases the value of your company, because to the rest of the world, you play well with others. There is the perception that by having institutional partners a company is run cleaner and more disciplined with timing management and financial reports.

An E-Recap to Buy Out One Partner

Often, we see one partner who wants out but the other partner really wants to keep going with the business. If we use the same example - the $10 million enterprise business and you had two owners that were 50/50, so each owner would have five million worth equity.

In the example we just used where we reached seven million which is really what happened in one transaction, we were able to get five million to the business owner that wanted to take that money off the table and go play golf.

The remaining owner was able to take two million off and still control 75% of the company. He went from owning 50% to 75% of the company and got two million out, and we got rid of the old partner. You can start seeing the power of this tool.

How E-Recap Differs from Private Equity and ESOP

What happened to Scott's friend is that the traditional private equity is where the private equity groups want majority control. The most of private equity groups that are out there on the market are looking for places to invest want majority control. In this case, the private equity group has that 75% and you have that 25% ownership. They have majority ownership of the company and equity, and they also then can tell you what to do, because in essence you are now really just working for them.

The other thing is, while you are working for them and you are getting the compensation, but the difference between the E-Recap where you own 75% versus a minority interest is over the next three, four, five years, you are going to get the economic benefit as the company pays down that leverage. For every dollar of debt paid down you are receiving 75% of the benefit verse 25%. Because you have the majority ownership you are getting the benefit because you maintained majority ownership. The leverage and the power really go to the entrepreneur by maintaining the majority ownership and that is why we call it the E-Recap, because we refer to it as the Entrepreneur Recap.

The Best of Both Worlds

One of the things that were eye-opening for us is that of course it makes sense to take capital off the table and have my financial freedom number met.

However, it also makes sense to me to invest that capital in a fairly stable and safer way than maintaining all our risk in my business. Doing that, we might yield between four and six percent, which is reasonable for a stable-type portfolio.

The challenge is that most business owners are getting 15 to 20 percent existing returns in their business. The problem is they could not sell it for enough to justify that number. The beauty of the E-Recap versus some other equity transaction is, we can take the number off my financial freedom number - invest it in a way that I'm diversifying my assets ideally at a lower-risk environment or a lower-risk investment strategy - yet still have a chunk in majority in this business at that 15-20% or so rate of return, and with growth, doing even better.

Many business owners then say, "Well, how do I get additional capital to grow since we have taken all the capital off the table?" We have an institutional partner that has already lent us money, and is an equity owner; they would lend more money for an acquisition or an increase in line. By going to the institutional business source - their private money - and they are willing to put more money in because they have a vested interest in the growth of the company.

In summary, with the private equity deal, traditionally, you have a minority position. On the other hand, an ESOP is highly regulated transaction with a lot of obligations; everyone is a shareholder, and so the compliance and the ongoing requirements of that compliance add a whole other layer of cost to things.

Who Are The Institutional Investors?

Once we come up with the plan of what the business owners want and what meet their needs, their financial freedom, or their objectives, we will go out and solicit from those institutional investors that are willing to do a minority type transaction and get multiple offers for the project. A good example of one is Main Street, a public company; they specialize on this side of the balance sheet.

What About the Cost of Debt?

The interest rate for the debt that we are putting on the business is going to be higher than the interest rate you would pay if you got it from a commercial bank. The difference is, the commercial bank is going to insist on your personal guarantee or they will lend it to you, but you cannot take it out of the business and put it in your personal bank account to diversify and invest it. It must only go back into the business.

The other thing is that they will have an amortization on that debt that will include principal. We try and get a non-amortizing debt component in this package, so the business can focus on the best use of that capital. You want to re-invest that money to grow; when you do that, you just pay the current interest rates. There is no pre-payment penalty, so if there is any excess cash at the end of the year, you can pay the debt off.

Another thing we frequently hear is, "The covenants are too restrictive. We won't be able to do anything." Again, because of the structure that we are proposing, that institution we borrowed the money from has ownership, so those restrictions are also affecting their capital. When you run the numbers, you can see the return on the capital for the institution, and they are all about helping you grow. Those are the two biggest things which we bundle up into the boogeyman effect; because they are making something bigger than it really is.

How Much Is Enough?

We will start by giving you a quote about financial freedom from Seneca: "It is not the man who has too little who is poor but the one who hungers after more. What difference does it make how much there is tucked away, how many head of stock he grazes or how much capital he puts out at interest? If he is always after what is another's and only counts what he has yet to get, never what he has already. You ask what the proper limit to a person's wealth is. First, having what is essential and second having what is enough."

Seneca passed in 65 AD, so these thoughts have been around awhile. The example of financial freedom that you may seek is complete financial independence to do whatever you want to do, in the lifestyle that you currently live. Independent of work, if you knew all of your payments would be met, your goals achieved, buying new vehicles, taking planned trips; if all of that was met; how much confidence would that bring you and your family?

That is what we mean by, "Financial freedom." It frees you up to really focus on the most meaningful areas in your life. For me, it is my six pillars, but that is what financial freedom means to me. Most business owners, we find, make this process much more difficult than it really is. You should do a comprehensive, thorough plan at some point to pinpoint what that number is, but it is not as complicated as most make it out to be.

As a business owner, take your salary and the bonuses that you take from your business, including what you run through your business. Add up everything to run your current lifestyle or ask your accountant to run it for you. Once you have that number, let us assume you are able to then invest a modern investment vehicle, lower risk in what your business currently is, and get a 5% rate of return out of that vehicle. You would then multiply that number by 20.

Of course, this is a hypothetical example and is not representative of any specific situation. Your results will vary. The hypothetical rates of return used do not reflect the deduction of fees and charges inherent to investing. Investing involves risk including loss of principal.

But for example, we will use $200,000 for easy numbers, as your annual expenses for the lifestyle you are currently living. If you multiply that number by 20, that means $4 million. So at $4 million at a 5% rate of return is giving you $200,000 or keeping and sustaining your current level or standard of living.

Clearly, doing a plan and delving deeper on exactly what the expenses are, factoring in inflation, factoring in taxes, etc. makes sense. But, the beauty with the E-Recap is that you are still going to have majority ownership in control and thus growth if the company continues to grow to have another future liquidity event down the road, and still collecting your salary for what you are doing in the company.

Clarity is the Key

That's a fairly straightforward, simplistic way to get a ballpark number. The problem is that when you ask business owners what their number is, they never can answer it. They do not have a clear-cut idea of what their number is, therefore, they cannot really make any kind of definitive plan, because they do not know where to start. This leads us back to why many of them have never done this type of planning in the first place.

As we stated earlier, so few business owners know the value of their business and very few have it well-planned or have any idea what this number needs to be or is in their situation. Warren Buffett and Bill Gates - pretty successful businessmen - were having dinner for the first time and they were asked about the number one reason for their success, and without reservation, Bill Gates said, "Laser focus." He asked Warren Buffet the same question and he said, "Getting clear on what the priority was, and focus." The bottom line both these men - some of the wealthiest men in the country - say the number one thing is focus.

It is kind of like buying a new car. Scott bought a Ford F-150 last year and it astounds him how many Ford F-150s that are out there, but you do not really recognize it until you are the one buying the car. Why? Because your subconscious is now looking for something it wasn't looking for before. It is amazing how your subconscious goes to work at looking on how to get you to that number. Clarity is the key.

Another Real Life Example

While working with business owners, once we become clear on that number, their decisions become easier because they understand why they are making those decisions. We remember one very small business, a gentleman wanted to retire, and he had a number of hard decisions that he was putting off.

He was carrying people that he should not have been carrying, and he had some product lines that he should not have been carrying because profit was not there. He cleaned that up and a number of fun things actually happened when he let go over the troubling employees; everyone's morale went up. Then when everyone's morale went up, the success of the business went up.

When they got rid of the non-profitable lines of business, then he also found out that people were not having enjoyment in selling those anyway, because they were not commissioned. The sales went up, and everyone's focus went up. By knowing your number, knowing that road map or where you are headed to, it starts picking up speed. Balance leads to growth and growth leads to balance. It's a virtuous cycle.

Is Financial Freedom Closer Than You Think?

Another myth we encounter often is most people think their financial freedom number is much bigger than it needs to be. When they follow our simple formula or do a more thorough plan, the number comes out to be much less than what they anticipated.

The reason for that is twofold. Some people have big dreams, and they do not want to give those up. But we ask about what they really want. It's typically a feeling that they are after, such as security. For example someone may say, "I would like to own a plane." The question becomes, "Why do you want to own a plane?" Well, the freedom of being able to go wherever I want to go when I want to go and do it in style. Well, what if, instead of owning the plane, you could still have freedom, you could still do it in style, and you could do it by leasing that plane, at 10% to 25% the cost of owning?

When you really get to the root of what you are trying to accomplish, and then figure out what it is really going to cost, the number historically comes back less than what they anticipate it to be.

Mistakes Business Owners Make Cashing Out

One of the mistakes we see are business owners being too rash and too quick to go into illiquid investments. They have just spent their entire lives building this company, which is illiquid the entire time. Then, for the first time, these people end up with this pile of cash, which is liquid; this is part of why we are doing this - to diversify. But because they are business owners, they typically have what we call "this next shiny object syndrome". They must learn to put this mindset aside. They need to stay liquid.

They start chasing the next shiny object and end up putting it into an illiquid investment or an illiquid business going into something too quickly. The second mistake we would mention is, not being safe enough with your investments. Part of why we do this is for diversification and to diversify a high risk asset into a lower risk asset. To do that, you need to put it in the something more diversified than what it was, not in your business.

One of the benefits of E-Recap is it's not an all or nothing, compared to Scott's friend who had really sold the majority of his business. Under the E-Recap, you still have your business and majority control. You are still operating it and you are receiving all those benefits.

One of the best places to use the E-Recap is ahead of time, and by using it five-seven years before, you ultimately exit the business. That way, you avoid the mistake we often see, which is having no plan at all. Prior to that, the business owner maybe had a $100,000 or $200,000 in an IRA or retirement plan, because every dollar they had was in that business.

If they do not have a plan, they do not know the path and the roadway to where they are going. They will invest it in a way that isn't wise or they will invest it in all in the next great real estate deal. Or worse, they will buy a restaurant, and they have never been in the restaurant business, they have always been in the construction business. You need a plan, and that's why we think this is really helpful, to overcome the biggest mistake we see of having no plan.

Is an E-Recap Right for You?

Each situation is very unique. Each business is unique. They all have unique growth rates, customer concentration products. The first thing that happens is they take a survey to see how they score, because this process is for businesses of a certain size, and with certain objectives. After taking that survey, then we should have a conversation and just expand on what those objectives are.

We also have available a simple straightforward assessment that helps them determine what is their financial freedom number, so they get clarity and it is not so daunting. They can go here for more information **www.cashingoutbook.com** or they can email us at **scottf@cornerstonewealthgroup.com**.

What If You Could Take Significant Cash Out of Your Business While Maintaining Majority Ownership?

If you are like most business owners, your business is your largest asset. This often presents several problems, including increased financial risk and lack of liquidity. Business owners frequently struggle to achieve true financial freedom without withdrawing funds from their company. Many owners dream of taking cash from their business but are not ready to give up ownership or control.

Traditional methods to cash out of a business often mean losing majority ownership and saddling your business with excess debt. That's where Cashing Out of Your Business comes in. The Cashing Out process used to be reserved for companies worth $50 million or more but is now available for companies valued at $10 million or greater. The method helps business owners like you remove cash from your business while keeping operational control and maintaining majority ownership.

Could an E-Recap be right for your business? Take the Cash Out Readiness Assessment to help determine if you and your company are a fit for the E-RECAP process at **cashingoutbook.com**.

Disclosures

E-Recap transactions present unique benefits and risks that must be evaluated. For more information on the E-Recap transaction, visit our website to learn more and contact us today to discuss how the process may be able to help your firm. There is no guarantee that diversification will enhance overall returns or outperform a non-diversified investment. Diversification does not protect against market risk. No strategy assures a profit or protects from loss. Investing involves risk, including loss of principal. Scott Ford do not provide business or financial valuations.